THE
DA VINCI
CODE

a response

THE
DA VINCI
CODE

a response

NICKY GUMBEL

Alpha International
London

Copyright © Nicky Gumbel 2005
The right of Nicky Gumbel to be identified as the author
of this work has been asserted by him in accordance with the
Copyright, Designs and Patents Act 1988.
This edition reprinted 2006

All rights reserved.
No part of this publication may be reproduced
or transmitted in any form or by any means,
electronic or mechanical, including photocopy,
recording or any information storage and
retrieval system, without permission
in writing from the publisher.

Unless otherwise stated, biblical quotations are from the
NEW INTERNATIONAL VERSION
© 1973, 1978, 1984 by
International Bible Society.
Inclusive Language Version 1995, 1996.

ISBN 1 904074 81 2

Published by Alpha International
Holy Trinity Brompton
Brompton Road
London SW7 1JA

Contents

1. Who does Dan Brown think Jesus is? — 3

2. Who did the first Christians think Jesus was? — 18

3. What did Jesus say about himself? — 30

4. What evidence is there to support what Jesus says? — 39

   Conclusion — 50

   Notes — 54

According to *The Daily Telegraph*, *The Da Vinci Code* is 'The biggest selling adult hardback fiction book of all time'.[1] It has sold millions of copies, been translated into dozens of languages and has been made into a $100 million film starring Tom Hanks and Ian McKellen, scheduled for release in May 2006. The book has made its author, Dan Brown, a multi-millionaire.

The New York Times described it as a 'riddle-filled, code-breaking, exhilarating, brainy thriller'.[2] There has been some debate about its literary merits. One critic concedes it is 'a superb thriller'.[3] Others have been less flattering. One book describes it as 'pretentious, posturing, self-serving, arrogant, self-congratulatory, condescending, glib, illogical, superficial, and deviant'.[4]

Whilst there may be debate about its literary merits, there is no doubt about the book's impact. One member of our congregation, at Holy Trinity Brompton in London, wrote down some of the comments people had made to her about *The Da Vinci Code*. A friend who was not sympathetic to Christianity said, 'It shows that the Bible can't possibly be accurate and that the text was changed'. Of her Christian friends, one said, 'It nearly made me lose my faith'. Another said, 'It made me think I don't have any real facts to back up my faith'.

How can a novel – a work of fiction – have such an impact? *The Da Vinci Code* is a thriller presented as a historical novel; it is fiction and yet seeks to convince the reader that it is based on fact. In the words of Cardinal George, Archbishop of Chicago, it is 'preposterous, but for many it is persuasive'.[5]

So what is it all about? We need not trouble ourselves with the plot, as in many respects, it is largely irrelevant to the theological assertions. This is not the place to examine the accuracy of the descriptions of the various places mentioned, such as Chateau de Villette near Paris, the Ritz Hotel, the Louvre museum, the Temple Church and many others. Although their mention has led to an increase in visits to these sights, the accuracy of the descriptions has been called into question. I do not have space to consider side issues such as the Knights Templar, The Priory of Sion or the works of Leonardo Da Vinci; nor to comment on the book's attacks on the Catholic Church ('The Vatican') and Opus Dei.

The root and foundation of *The Da Vinci Code* is theological. In fact, it is Christological. The whole edifice is built on a theory about who Jesus was and is, and the rest of the story only becomes relevant if there is anything in that theory.

We will first look at the specific claims *The Da Vinci Code* makes about Jesus (Part 1), then we will consider the view of the early Christians (Part 2), the way Jesus saw himself (Part 3), and the evidence that supports what he said (Part 4).

PART ONE

❦

Who does Dan Brown think Jesus is?

1.1. What is the central premise of *The Da Vinci Code*?

Through its characters, *The Da Vinci Code* asserts that *'almost everything our fathers taught us about Christ is false'*.[6] It claims that:

- The Catholic Church has kept the true facts about Christianity hidden through force and terror
- Jesus was married to Mary Magdalene (who was the head apostle)
- The Holy Grail is not, as commonly believed, the chalice used at the last supper but the womb of Mary Magdalene who bore Jesus' daughter, Sarah
- The descendants of Mary Magdalene and Jesus became Kings of France[7]
- Jesus was not the Son of God
- He was a mortal prophet – a great and powerful man of staggering influence who inspired millions to live better lives
- Jesus was a radical feminist
- The pagan emperor Constantine proposed a motion to upgrade Jesus to a deity at the Council of Nicaea in 325AD
- Jesus became the Son of God by a narrow vote, but that prior to that, no one believed him to be divine
- Constantine's motive was to give power to the Roman Catholic Church.

How does Dan Brown reach this conclusion? The argument has two parts: first, that the earliest Christian records do not match up with the Bible, and second, that Constantine collated the Bible as we now have it. It is claimed that Constantine commissioned and financed a new Bible, which omitted those gospels that spoke of Christ's human traits and embellished those depicting him as godlike. According to *The Da Vinci Code*, Constantine rejected dozens of other 'gospels' and rewrote the four that are in the Bible today. It claims that thousands of 'gospels' were burnt or outlawed but that some survived – for example Q, the Dead Sea Scrolls and the Nag Hammadi documents.

The Da Vinci Code suggests that the church has been hiding the real truth about Jesus and that this is the greatest conspiracy and cover-up of the last 2,000 years. It claims that rumours of this conspiracy have been whispered for centuries in countless languages, especially through the media of art, music, literature and, most dramatically, in the paintings of Leonardo Da Vinci. The book alleges that the secret remains protected to this day by a clandestine brotherhood, of which Da Vinci was a member. In summary, the book suggests that Christianity as we know it is a gigantic fraud.

1.2. Does Dan Brown himself believe all this to be true?

Here there is a certain ambivalence. The novel starts with a 'fact page' which ends by claiming, 'All descriptions of artwork, architecture, documents and secret rituals in this novel are accurate'.[8] Presumably this includes the New Testament documents and the other documents which refer to Jesus. It is possible that some readers might interpret this to mean that the conclusions he comes to about Jesus also have some basis in 'fact'.

Dan Brown's website states that it is 'my belief that the theories discussed by these characters may have merit'. He does not actually state that they are accurate or true but he disagrees with those who attempt to disprove *The Da Vinci Code*. He describes himself as a Christian but distinguishes himself from those who accept 'the Bible as absolute historical fact'. He says 'We're each following our own path of enlightenment. I consider myself a student of many religions'.[9]

1.3. What is *The Da Vinci Code's* evidence?

Is there any evidence for an earlier version of Christianity than the one which is described in the New

Testament? *The Da Vinci Code* cites three sources, bracketing them together as, 'The earliest Christian records'.[10] It claims:

> Some of the gospels that Constantine attempted to eradicate managed to survive. The Dead Sea Scrolls were found in the 1950s hidden in a cave near Qumran in the Judean desert. And, of course, the Coptic Scrolls in 1945 at Nag Hammadi. In addition to telling the true Grail story, these documents speak of Christ's ministry in very human terms. The scrolls highlight glaring historical discrepancies and fabrications, clearly confirming that the modern Bible was compiled and edited by men who possessed a political agenda – to promote the divinity of the man Jesus Christ and use His influence to solidify their own power base.[11]

Thirdly, *The Da Vinci Code* cites 'the legendary "Q" Document – a manuscript that even the Vatican admit they believe exists. Allegedly, it is a book of Jesus' teachings, possibly written in His own hand'.[12]

Do the claims about these three sources have any basis in fact?

i. Q

All that is new here is the suggestion that Q was written by Jesus. Q is the hypothetical source of those passages of the synoptic Gospels where Matthew and

Luke show a close similarity to each other but not to anything in Mark. It consists largely of sayings of Jesus. These came to be referred to by German scholars as Quelle (meaning 'source'). In the twentieth century, the Q hypothesis was the basis of nearly all serious study of the origin and development of the Gospel traditions.

Whether or not Q exists as a document is – to some extent – irrelevant. The whole point is that we know, roughly speaking, what was in Q from the Gospels of Matthew and Luke. So there is nothing here to shake our confidence in the documents which we already have in the New Testament. Q adds nothing to what we already have in the New Testament and certainly does not contradict the existing Gospels.

ii. The Dead Sea Scrolls

These were found from 1947 onwards near Qumran. They contained three things:

1. All of the Old Testament books except Esther – for example, the oldest copy of Isaiah by 1000 years
2. Biblical commentaries on Old Testament books, psalms and hymns
3. Sectarian material belonging to the Qumran community itself.

It is true that delays in publication led to conspiracy theories that the Scrolls contained information that would undermine Christianity. However, it is no longer possible to assert this as there is no textual evidence to support the claim. All the Dead Sea Scrolls have been translated into English and can be purchased at any good bookshop. These are not Gospels at all. There is no mention of Jesus, Paul or John the Baptist. They contain very interesting background information about the New Testament, but bear no direct relationship to it. Far from being the earliest Christian records, they are not Christian records at all.

iii. The Nag Hammadi documents

In 1945 two peasant farmers in Upper Egypt came across a jar as they were digging. They smashed the jar thinking it might contain gold. Inside they found papyrus codices. One of them, Muhammed Ali, wrapped the books in his tunic, got on his camel and carried them back to a tiny hovel in his hamlet. When the documents eventually came to light, they were found to be fourth century Coptic papyrus manuscripts. There were 12 codices (ancient manuscripts) and eight leaves from a thirteenth century codex. They contained 45 separate titles written in Coptic which had been translated from Greek. They provide a Gnostic library which is the single most important contribution towards our knowledge of Gnosticism.

Gnosticism is a very difficult movement to define, rather like the New Age movement today. It was esoteric, decentralised and eclectic and was the greatest challenge to the fledgling Christian faith of the second and third centuries. There were endless varieties of Gnosticism, but at heart there was a radical dualism between the spiritual and the material. The material realm was regarded as evil. From the unknowable 'Supreme Being' proceeded a series of emanations or 'aeons' – exalted spiritual beings capable of a measure of communication with the 'Supreme Being'. One of the lower 'aeons' who had no direct contact with the 'Supreme Being' was responsible for Creation. Thus, the creation, if not positively evil was, at least, clumsy and ignorant – a sphere from which human beings must escape.

The only way of escape was 'gnosis' – the secret knowledge of the true god. Salvation was thought to be about overcoming ignorance through self knowledge. The function of the Christ was to come as an emissary of the supreme God, bringing 'gnosis'. As a divine being, he neither assumed a fully human body, nor did he die. He either temporarily inhabited a human being, Jesus, or assumed a merely phantasmal human appearance.

Gnosticism tended to be docetic. Docetism comes from the Greek word dokeo meaning 'I seem'. It is a tendency which considered the humanity and sufferings of the earthly Christ as apparent rather than real (ie

Jesus only seemed to be a real human being). It is a heresy which is attacked in the New Testament itself (see 1 John 4:1–3, 2 John 7 and Colossians 2:8 ff). Although it was beginning to appear in New Testament times, it reached its zenith in the next generation – especially among the Gnostics.

Our knowledge of Gnosticism was greatly increased by the discovery of the Nag Hammadi documents. There is no 'secret' about what was found at Nag Hammadi (as implied by *The Da Vinci Code*). Again, a copy can be bought at any large bookshop.

The Nag Hammadi documents are not really Gospels at all. The Gnostic 'gospels' are non-historical, and even anti-historical, with little narrative or sense of chronology. They were written generations after the facts whilst claiming direct, secret knowledge about them. Much of it is pseudepigrapha which is at best a literary device, and at worst a fraud. For example, the gospel of Thomas claims to have been written by the apostle Thomas when it cannot possibly have been, as he had probably been dead for decades, if not centuries by the time they were written.

The anti-Gnostic writers such as Irenaeus, Tertullian and Hippolytus emphasise the pagan features of Gnosticism and appeal to the plain sense of Scripture – as interpreted by the tradition of the church – which had been handed down by a chain of teachers reaching back to the apostles. They insisted on the identity of the Creator and Supreme God, on the goodness of the material of creation and on the reality of the earthly life of Jesus, especially his crucifixion and resurrection. They asserted that human beings need redemption from evil, rather than from an evil environment.

The Da Vinci Code cites three of the Gnostic 'gospels' as evidence:

i. The 'gospel' of Thomas

This is a Coptic version written around 400AD, translated from the original Greek (probably written around 150AD). It is not like the canonical Gospels. It is historical in form, but consists of a series of pithy sayings and parabolic discourses of Jesus – for example, the parables of the sower, the mustard seed, the tenants and the lost sheep and various sayings from the Sermon on the Mount. In addition, it includes other sayings which show signs of Gnosticism.

It is ironic that *The Da Vinci Code* claims that Jesus was more sympathetic to women than the New Testament documents suggest and that there is evidence of this in these other documents. In fact, Gnostic anthropology had a very low view of women. They were regarded as secondary and defective beings. For example, the 'gospel' of Thomas ends with saying 114:

> Simon Peter said to them, "Let Mary leave us, for women are not worthy of life."
>
> Jesus said, "I myself shall lead her in order to make her male, so that she too may become a living spirit resembling you males. For every woman who will make herself male will enter the kingdom of heaven." [13]

In other words, the only way for a woman to be saved is to become a man. This is hardly radical feminism! In the context of his era, the Jesus of the New Testament shows a far more enlightened and revolutionary view of the dignity, status and equality of women. He challenged the patriarchy of his day. He spoke to a Samaritan woman in public, he travelled with women disciples, and he chose to have women amongst his closest friends. Jesus' teaching in the New Testament directly challenges the Gnostic view of salvation being dependent upon females becoming male. He said of judgement: 'Two men will be in the field; one will be taken and the other left. Two women will be grinding with a hand mill; one will be taken and the other left' (Matthew 24:40 42). In other words he said judgement would be made not on the basis of gender, but rather on the basis of faith.

ii. The 'gospel' of Philip

This is another of the Gnostic treaties found at Nag

Hammadi. It contains no narrative but only a few incidents and sayings attributed to Christ. It may well have been written as late as the second half of the third century.

This 'gospel' contains the passage on which *The Da Vinci Code* relies for the suggestion that Jesus was married to Mary Magdalene:

> And the companion of the... Mary Magdalene. ...loved her more than all the disciples and used to kiss her [often] on her... The rest of the disciples... They said to him, "Why do you love her more than all of us?" [14]

iii. The 'gospel' of Mary

This again belongs to the genre of the Gnostic dialogue. It was originally written in Greek some time in the second century. The passage which *The Da Vinci Code* relies on says:

> And Peter said, "Did the Saviour really speak with a woman without our knowledge? Are we to turn about and all listen to her? Did he prefer her to us?"
>
> And Levi answered, "Peter, you have always been hot-tempered. Now I see you contending against the woman like an adversary. If the Saviour made her worthy, who are you indeed to reject her? Surely the Saviour knows her very well. That is why he loved her more than us." [15]

From these, a conclusion is drawn that, 'According to these unaltered gospels, it was not *Peter* to whom Christ gave directions with which to establish the Christian Church. It was *Mary Magdalene*.'[16] As we see in the passage above, this is not even what the so called 'gospel' of Mary suggests.

1.4. Is there any evidence that Jesus was married to Mary Magdalene?

There are at least a dozen references to Mary from Magdala (a town on the western shore of the Sea of Galilee) in the four Gospels of the New Testament (Matthew, Mark, Luke and John):

- She is described as a woman who had suffered from demonic possession and from whom Jesus expelled seven demons (Mark 16:9; Luke 8:2)
- She is one of the women who accompanied Jesus in his ministry (Luke 8:2)
- She was a witness of the crucifixion (Matthew 27:56; Mark 15:40; John 19:25)
- She was present at the burial of Jesus (Matthew 27:61; Mark 15:47)
- She was a witness of the empty tomb (Matthew 28:1–10; Mark 16:1–8; Luke 24:10)
- After his resurrection, Jesus appeared to her alone at the tomb (Mark 16:9; John 20:1–18).

However, throughout Scripture we find not a trace of evidence to suggest that Jesus ever married. During his teaching, a wife is never mentioned. At his trial and subsequent crucifixion, a wife is never mentioned. There is no suggestion of a wife or a marriage at any point of Jesus' life. Even the Gnostic 'gospels', taken at face value, do not suggest that Jesus was married, let alone that he had a child. It is interesting to compare another Gnostic text, the Second Apocalypse of James, which describes the risen Jesus imparting his secret mysteries to James by kissing him on the mouth and calling him 'my beloved'. This is a non-sexual symbolic act. However, the incident bears striking similarities to the extract in the 'gospel' of Philip, alleged to provide evidence of Jesus' marriage to Mary Magdalene. Further, the 'gospel' of Philip was probably written 250 years after the events it describes, bears no relationship to historical reality and is regarded by scholars as an allegory of the relationship of Christ and his church.

Indeed, while *The Da Vinci Code* suggests that these Gnostic 'gospels' were earlier than the New Testament documents, the 'gospel' of Philip actually quotes from the New Testament, (eg 1 Corinthians 8:1, 1 Peter 4:8, Matthew 15:13). This surely is good evidence that the 'gospel' of Philip was written after the New Testament and not before.

There is, therefore, not a shred of historical evidence that Jesus married Mary Magdalene. Even more fanciful is the suggestion that between them they gave birth to a daughter and that their descendants were kings of France. This is indeed pure fiction.

PART TWO

Who did the first Christians think Jesus was?

2.1. Is there any evidence for this 'earlier form of Christianity' when 'no one believed Jesus was divine'?

The Da Vinci Code suggests that prior to 325AD – and Constantine's intervention – no one believed Jesus was divine:

> Constantine commissioned and financed a new Bible, which omitted those gospels that spoke of Christ's human traits and embellished those gospels that made Him godlike. The earlier gospels were outlawed, gathered up, and burned. ... Fortunately for historians... some of the gospels that Constantine attempted to eradicate managed to survive. The Dead Sea Scrolls were found in the 1950's hidden in a cave near Qumran in the Judean desert. And, of course, the Coptic Scrolls in 1945 at Nag Hammadi. In addition to telling the true Grail story, these documents speak of Christ's ministry in very human terms.[17]

In fact the very opposite was the case. It was the Gnostic gospels that 'omitted Christ's human traits' and 'embellished' the earlier accounts to make him more 'godlike'. This is one of the many reasons the Gnostic gospels were excluded from the earlier canon. The New Testament assumes the full humanity of Jesus. He had a human body; he was sometimes tired (John 4:6) and hungry (Matthew 4:2). He had human emotions: he was angry (Mark 11:15–17), he loved (Mark 10:21) and he was sad (John 11:35). He had human experiences: he was tempted (Mark 1:13), he learned (Luke 2:52), he worked (Mark 6:3) and he obeyed his parents (Luke 2:51). The New Testament writers dealt very firmly with anyone who suggested that Jesus was not fully human (see 1 John 4:1–3, 2 John 7, Col 2:8 ff).

Therefore, the facts are the very opposite to those suggested in *The Da Vinci Code*. The New Testament does not omit the Gospels that speak of Christ's human traits – otherwise it would have left out Matthew, Mark, Luke and John. Ironically, it is the Gnostic 'gospels' which tend to omit his human traits. Unlike the New Testament they tend to be docetic and do not speak of Christ's ministry in very human terms.

Further, it is not true to say that 'prior to 325AD no one believed Jesus was divine'. Analysis of the textual families of the orthodox Gospels and comparison with fragments and quotations, coupled with historical correlations, seemingly put their date in the first century, thus indicating that they are far earlier than the Gnostic forgeries. The epistles of St Paul are, of course, even earlier than the Gospels. Paul was a historical figure and contemporary of Jesus, and his letters date from as early as 48AD. Paul writes for example, 'One Lord, Jesus Christ, through whom all things came' (1 Corinthians 8:6) and, 'He is the image of the invisible God. By him all things were created' (Colossians 1:15–16).

However, we do not even need to turn to the New Testament to prove that Christians believed Jesus was more than a mere mortal long before the time of Constantine. In 112AD, the Roman governor Pliny records that 'Christians were in the habit of meeting regularly before dawn on a fixed date to chant verses alternately among themselves in honour of Christ as to a God.'[18] It is clear that the early church worshipped Jesus as God from the very earliest days.

Furthermore, numerous church fathers speak of the divinity of Christ. For example:

- Ignatius (CA 50–CA 117) 'our God, Jesus Christ'[19]
- Justin Martyr (CA 100–CA 165) 'He was God'[20]
- Melito of Sardis (died CA 190) 'Being God and likewise perfect man'[21]
- Irenaeus (CA 130–CA 200) 'He is the holy Lord, the Wonderful, the Counsellor... and the Mighty God'[22]
- Clement of Alexandria (CA 150–CA 215) 'He alone is both God and man'[23]
- Tertullian (CA 160–CA 225) 'for Christ is also God.'[24]

In his seminal work 'Early Christian Doctrines', eminent church historian Dr J.N.D. Kelly, writes:

> The all but universal Christian conviction in the preceding centuries (to Nicaea) had been that Jesus Christ was divine as well as human. The most primitive confession

had been 'Jesus is Lord', and its import had been elaborated and deepened in the apostolic age. The New Testament writers generally regarded Christ as pre-existent; they tended to attribute to Him a twofold order of being, 'according to the flesh', i.e. as man, and 'according to Spirit', i.e. as God. So deeply was this formula embedded in their thinking that...it (is) 'the foundation datum of all later Christological development'. [25]

The Da Vinci Code fails to produce a shred of credible evidence of an earlier form of Christianity in which 'no one believed Jesus was divine'. The historical evidence is all to the contrary. From the very earliest days Jesus was seen as divine and worshipped as God by the early church.

2.2. What happened at Nicaea and what was Constantine's role?

The Da Vinci Code claims that, 'Jesus' establishment as 'the Son of God' was officially proposed and voted on by the Council of Nicaea' – ie Jesus' divinity was the result of a vote and, 'A relatively close vote at that'.[26] But it is certainly not true that Constantine 'upgraded' Jesus to a deity at the Council of Nicaea.[27] Constantine did summon the Council of Nicaea but it is not true that 'He was a lifelong pagan who was baptised on his deathbed, too weak to protest,' as alleged in *The Da Vinci Code*.[28]

Constantine's policy was to unite the Christian church to the secular state. He did his best to reconcile both pagans and Christians. It is difficult to say when he was converted. It is true he was not baptised until shortly before his death – but the deferment of baptism was common in those days. His policies were strongly Christian from the first. He humanised the criminal laws and law of debt. He mitigated the conditions of slavery and made grants to support poor children. He discouraged the exposure of unwanted babies. He freed celibates and unmarried people from special taxes and legislated against promiscuity. In 321AD he ordered that Sundays should become public holidays.

Constantine summoned the Council of Nicaea primarily to end disunity and controversy caused by the Arian controversy. Arius taught that although Jesus was the Son of God he was less than the Father, a lesser god. (The nearest equivalent teaching might be that of the Jehovah's Witnesses today.) The Council of Nicaea was opened by Constantine and then he passed on the presidency. His main aim was to secure unity rather than any predetermined theological verdict. The Council was probably attended by 220–250 bishops. The Arian creed was rejected and they produced the Nicene Creed with four anti-Arian anathemas attached. This was accepted by all but two of the bishops – that is, over ninety-nine per cent were in favour. They declared that Jesus was the

Son of God 'begotten not made, of the same substance (homo-ousios) as the Father'. [29]

It is totally untrue that 'until that moment in history, Jesus was viewed by His followers as a mortal prophet... a great and powerful man, but a man none the less. A mortal.' [30] In fact Jesus had been regarded as the Son of God from the very beginning. The discussion at Nicaea was not about whether he was the Son of God or a mere 'mortal'. The only thing everybody agreed on was that Jesus was more than mortal. It was about whether he was the same substance as the Father or a lesser God. The vote was not 'relatively close'[30] but an overwhelming majority in favour of the orthodox creed.

Nor is it true to say that, 'The Bible, as we know it today, was collated by the pagan Roman emperor Constantine the Great.' [31] The emperor Constantine had absolutely nothing to do with fixing the Canon of Scripture. The Canon was pretty well fixed by the fourth century – although it was more a case of the church publishing for the sake of clarity what it had (subject to minor variations) always believed to be true. Its kernel of the four Gospels and thirteen letters of Paul had come to be accepted by around 130AD and was placed on the same footing as the Old Testament between 170 and 220AD. The Muratorian fragment (c170AD) demonstrates that sixty-one out of the sixty-six books of our Bible were already treated as sacred 100 years before Constantine was born. Agreement of the final list of books and the order in which they were arranged was the result of a very gradual process. The criterion which ultimately came to prevail was apostolicity. Unless a book could be shown to come from the pen of an apostle, or at least have the authority of an apostle behind it, it was rejected. In gradual stages, both the Eastern and Western Church arrived at a common mind as to its sacred books. The late Professor F. F. Bruce, former Rylands Professor of biblical criticism and exegesis at the University of Manchester, points out:

> One thing must be emphatically stated. The New Testament books did not become authoritative for the Church because they were formally included in a canonical list; on the contrary, the Church included them in her canon because she already regarded them as divinely inspired, recognising their innate worth and generally apostolic authority, direct or indirect. The first ecclesiastical councils to classify the canonical books were both held in North Africa – at Hippo Regius in 393 and at Carthage in 397 – but what these councils did was not to impose something new upon the Christian communities but to codify what was already the general practice of those communities. [32]

The Gnostic 'gospels' were never among the books considered for the Canon by the early church. They were written a century too late to be written by the people they name (eg Thomas, Philip or Mary Magdalene). Even the second century leader, Marcion, did not list these as part of his canon but only the books found in our current New Testament. This is the strongest possible evidence that the so-called 'Gnostic gospels' did not exist at that stage.

Further, it is absurd to suggest that Constantine 'embellished' the Gospels that we have. We know that they have not been changed through the science of textual criticism. Essentially the more texts we have, the less doubt there is about the original. In his book *Are the New Testament Documents Reliable?*, Professor F.F. Bruce shows how wealthy the New Testament is in manuscript attestation by comparing its texts with other historical works.

The table below summarise the facts and shows the extent of the New Testament evidence.

Work	When written	Earliest copy	Time span (yrs)	No. of copies
Herodotus	488-428BC	900AD	1,300	8
Thucydides	c. 460-400BC	c. 900AD	1,300	8
Tacitus	100AD	1100	1,000	20
Caesar's Gallic War	58-50BC	900AD	950	9-10
Livy's Roman History	59 BC-AD 17	900AD	900	20
New Testament	40-100AD	130AD (full manuscripts 350AD)	300	5,000+ Greek 10,000 Latin 9,300 others

F.F Bruce points out that for Caesar's *Gallic War* we have nine or ten copies and the oldest was written some 900 years later than Caesar's day. For Livy's *Roman History* we have not more than twenty copies, the earliest of which comes from around 900AD. Of the fourteen books of the histories of Tacitus only twenty copies survive; of the sixteen books of his *Annals*, ten portions of his two great historical works depend entirely on two manuscripts, one of the ninth century and one of the eleventh century. The history of Thucydides is known almost entirely from eight manuscripts belonging to c 900AD. The same is true of the history of Herodutus. Yet no classical scholar doubts the authenticity of these works, in spite of the large time gap and the relatively small number of manuscripts.

As regards the New Testament, we have a great wealth of material. The New Testament was probably written between 40AD and 100AD. We have some parchments which date from before 325AD (the time of Constantine's intervention, and a time span of less than 300 years), papyri containing most of the New Testament writings dating from the third century, and even a fragment of John's Gospel, which was dated on paleographic grounds around 130AD. These can be seen in the John Rylands library in Manchester. Considerable fragments remain of papyrus copies of books of the New Testament from the 2nd and 3rd century, eg the Chester Beatty biblical papyri. Many early manuscripts can be seen in libraries and museums around the world.

In all there are over 5,000 Greek manuscripts, over 10,000 Latin manuscripts and 9,300 other manuscripts, as well as over 36,000 citings in the writings of the early church fathers. As one of the greatest ever textual critics, F.J.A. Hort, said, 'In the variety and fullness of the evidence on which it rests, the text of the New Testament stands absolutely and unapproachably alone among other ancient prose writings.' [33]

F.F Bruce summarises the evidence by quoting Sir Frederic Kenyon, a leading scholar in this area:

> The interval then between the dates of original composition and the earliest extant evidence becomes so small as to be in fact negligible, and the last foundation for any doubt that the Scriptures have come down to us substantially as they were written has now been removed. Both the *authenticity* and the general *integrity* of the books of the New Testament may be regarded as finally established. [34]

It therefore seems absolutely clear that the existing manuscripts have not been embellished either by Constantine or by anyone else.

The Da Vinci Code does not produce a shred of credible evidence for an earlier form of Christianity to that which we find in our New Testament. If *The Da Vinci Code* only claims to be a novel that is fine. If it claims to be based on scholarship, it is fanciful, absurd and in the end ridiculous. It is another 'myth' – a twenty-first century Gnostic myth.

PART THREE

What did Jesus say about himself?

I am told that in a communist Russian dictionary Jesus is described as 'a mythical figure who never existed'. No serious historian could maintain that position today. There is a great deal of evidence for Jesus' existence. This comes not only from the Gospels and other Christian writings, but also from non-Christian sources. For example, the Roman historians Tacitus (directly) and Suetonius (indirectly) both write about him. The Jewish historian Josephus, born in 37AD, describes Jesus and his followers thus:

> Now there was about this time, Jesus, a wise man, if it be lawful to call him a man, for he was a doer of wonderful works – a teacher of such men as receive the truth with pleasure. He drew over to him both many of the Jews, and many of the Gentiles. He was [the] Christ; and when Pilate, at the suggestion of the principal men amongst us, had condemned him to the cross, those that loved him at first did not forsake him, for he appeared to them alive again the third day, as the divine prophets had foretold these and ten thousand other wonderful things concerning him; and the tribe of Christians so named after him, are not extinct to this day.[35]

So there is evidence, both inside and outside the New Testament, for the existence of Jesus. But who is he? Who did he say he was?

Some people say, 'Jesus never claimed to be God.' Indeed, it is true that Jesus did not go round saying the words 'I am God.' Yet when one looks at all he taught and claimed, there is little doubt that he was conscious of being a person whose identity was God.

3.1 Teaching centred on himself

One of the fascinating things about Jesus is that so much of his teaching was centred on himself. He said to people, in effect, 'If you want to have a relationship with God you need to come to me' (see John 14:6). It is through a relationship with him that we encounter God.

There is a hunger deep within the human heart. The leading psychologists of the twentieth century have all recognised this. Freud said 'People are hungry for love.' Jung said, 'People are hungry for security.' Adler said, 'People are hungry for significance.' Jesus said, 'I am the bread of life' (John 6:35). In other words, 'If you want your hunger satisfied, come to me.'

Many people are walking in darkness, depression, disillusionment and despair. They are looking for direction. Jesus said, 'I am the light of the world. Whoever follows me will never walk in darkness, but will have the light of life' (John 8:12). Someone said to me after they had become a Christian, 'It was as if a light had suddenly been turned on and I could see things for the first time.'

Many are fearful of death. One woman said to me that sometimes she couldn't sleep and that she would wake up in a cold sweat, frightened about death, because she didn't know what was going to happen when she died. Jesus said, 'I am the resurrection and the life. Those who believe in me will live, even though they die; and whoever lives and believes in me will never die' (John 11:25-26).

So many are burdened by worries, anxieties, fears and guilt. Jesus said, 'Come to me, all you who are weary and burdened, and I will give you rest' (Matthew 11:28). They are not sure how to run their lives or who they should follow. I can remember, before I was a Christian, that I would be impressed by someone and want to be like them, and then by a different person and follow them. Jesus said, 'Follow me' (Mark 1:17).

He said to receive him was to receive God (Matthew 10:40), to welcome him was to welcome God (Mark 9:37) and to have seen him was to have seen God (John 14:9). A child once drew a picture and her mother asked her what she was doing. The child said, 'I am drawing a picture of God.' The mother said, 'Don't be silly. You can't draw a picture of God. No one knows what God looks like.' The child replied, 'Well, they will do by the time I have finished!' Jesus said in effect, 'If you want to know what God looks like, look at me.'

3.2 Indirect claims

Jesus said a number of things which, although not direct claims to be God, show that he regarded himself as being in the same position as God, as we will see in the examples that follow.

Jesus' claim to be able to forgive sins is well known. For example, on one occasion he said to a man who was paralysed, 'Son, your sins are forgiven' (Mark 2:5). The reaction of the religious leaders was, 'Why does this fellow talk like this? He's blaspheming! Who can forgive sins but God alone?' Jesus went on to prove that he did have the authority to forgive sins by healing the paralysed man. This claim to be able to forgive sins is indeed an astonishing claim.

C.S Lewis puts it well when he says in his book *Mere Christianity*:

> One part of the claim tends to slip past us unnoticed because we have heard it so often we no longer see what it amounts to. I mean the claim to forgive sins: any sins. Now unless the speaker is God, this is really so preposterous as to be comic. We can all understand how a man forgives offences against himself. You tread on my toes and I forgive you, you steal my money and I forgive you. But what should we make of a man, himself unrobbed and untrodden on, who announced that he forgave you for treading on other men's toes and stealing other men's money? Asinine fatuity is the kindest

description we should give of his conduct. Yet this is what Jesus did. He told people that their sins were forgiven, and never waited to consult all the other people whom their sins had undoubtedly injured. He unhesitatingly behaved as if He was the party chiefly concerned, the person chiefly offended in all offences. This makes sense only if He really was the God whose laws are broken and whose love is wounded in every sin. In the mouth of any speaker who is not God, these words would imply what I can only regard as a silliness and conceit unrivalled by any other character in history.[36]

Another extraordinary claim that Jesus made was that one day he would judge the world (Matthew 25:31-32). He said he would return and 'sit on his throne in heavenly glory' (v.31). All the nations would be gathered before him. He would pass judgement on them. Some would receive an inheritance prepared for them since the creation of the world and eternal life, but others would suffer the punishment of being separated from him for ever.

Jesus said he would decide what happens to every one of us at the end of time. Not only would he be the Judge, he would also be the criterion of judgement. What happens to us on the Day of Judgement depends on how we respond to Jesus in this life (Matthew 25:40, 45). Suppose the vicar of your local church was to get up in the pulpit and say, 'On the Day of Judgement you will all appear before me and I will decide your eternal destiny.

What happens to you will depend on how you've treated me and my followers.' For a mere human being to make such a claim would be preposterous. Here we have another indirect claim to have the identity of Almighty God.

3.3 Direct claims

When the question was put to him, 'Are you the Christ, the Son of the Blessed One?' Jesus said, 'I am... and you will see the Son of Man sitting at the right hand of the Mighty One and coming on the clouds of heaven.' The high priest tore his clothes. 'Why do we need any more witnesses?' he asked. 'You have heard the blasphemy. What do you think?' (Mark 14:61 – 64). In this account it appears Jesus was condemned to death for the assertion he made about himself. A claim tantamount to a claim to be God was blasphemy in Jewish eyes, worthy of death.

On one occasion, when the Jews started to stone Jesus, he asked, 'Why are you stoning me?' They replied that they were stoning him for blasphemy 'because you, a mere man, *claim to be God*' (John 10:33, italics mine). His enemies clearly thought that this was exactly what he was declaring.

When Thomas, one of his disciples, knelt down before Jesus and said, 'My Lord and my God' (John 20:28), Jesus didn't turn to him and say, 'No, no, don't say that; I am not God.' He said, 'Because you have seen me, you have believed; blessed are those who have not seen and yet have believed' (John 20:29). He rebuked Thomas for being so slow to get to the point.

If somebody makes claims like these they need to be tested. There are all sorts of people who make all kinds of claims. The mere fact that somebody claims to be someone does not mean that they are right. There are many people, some in psychiatric hospitals, who are deluded. They think they are Napoleon or the Pope, but they are not.

So how can we test people's claims? Jesus claimed to be the unique Son of God – God made flesh. There are three logical possibilities. If the claims were untrue, either he knew they were untrue – in which case he was an impostor, and an evil one at that. That is the first possibility. Or he did not know – in which case he was deluded; indeed, he was insane. That is the second possibility. The third possibility is that the claims were true.

C.S Lewis pointed out that: 'A man who was merely a man and said the sort of things that Jesus said would not be a great moral teacher.' He would either be insane or else he would be 'the Devil of Hell.' 'You must make your choice,' he writes. Either Jesus was, and is, the son of

God or else he was insane or evil but, C.S Lewis goes on, 'let us not come up with any patronising nonsense about His being a great human teacher. He has not left that open to us. He did not intend to.'[37]

PART FOUR

֍

What evidence is there to support what Jesus said?

In order to assess which of these three possibilities is right we need to examine the evidence we have about his life.

4.1 His teaching

The teaching of Jesus is widely acknowledged to be the greatest teaching that has ever fallen from human lips. Some who are not Christians say, 'I love the Sermon on the Mount; I live by it.' (If they were to read it they would realise that this is easier to say than to do, but they acknowledge that the Sermon on the Mount is great teaching).

Bernard Ramm, an American professor of theology, said this about the teachings of Jesus:

> They are read more, quoted more, loved more, believed more, and translated more because they are the greatest words ever spoken... Their greatness lies in the pure lucid spirituality in dealing clearly, definitively, and authoritatively with the greatest problems that throb in the human breast... No other man's words have the appeal of Jesus' words because no other man can answer these fundamental human questions as Jesus answered them. They are the kind of words and the kind of answers we would expect God to give.[38]

His teaching is the foundation of our entire civilisation in the West. Many of the laws in this country were originally based on the teachings of Jesus. We are making progress in virtually every field of science and technology. We travel faster and know more, and yet in nearly 2,000 years no one has improved on the moral teaching of Jesus Christ. Could that teaching really have come from someone evil or insane?

4.2 His works

Jesus said that the miracles he performed were in themselves evidence that 'the Father is in me, and I in the Father' (John 10:38).

Jesus must have been the most extraordinary person to have around. Sometimes people say that Christianity is boring. Well, it was not boring being with Jesus. When he went to a party, he turned water into wine (John 2:1-11). He received one man's picnic and multiplied it so that it could feed thousands (Mark 6:30-44). He had control over the elements and could speak to the wind and the waves and thereby stop a storm (Mark 4:35-41). He carried out the most remarkable healings: opening blind eyes, causing the deaf and dumb to hear and speak, and enabling the paralysed to walk again. When he visited a hospital a man who had been an invalid for thirty-eight years was able to pick up his bed and walk (John 5:1-9). He set people free from evil forces which had dominated their lives. On occasions, he even brought those who had died back to life (John 11:38-44).

Yet it was not just his miracles that made his work so impressive. It was his love, especially for the loveless (such as the lepers and the prostitutes), which seemed to motivate all that he did. The supreme demonstration of his love for us was shown on the cross (which was the chief reason for his coming to earth). When they tortured him and nailed him to the cross he said 'Father, forgive them, for they do not know what they are doing' (Luke 22:34). Surely these are not the activities of an evil or deluded man?

4.3 His character

The character of Jesus has impressed millions who would not call themselves Christians. For example, Bernard Levin wrote of Jesus:

> Is not the nature of Christ, in the words of the New Testament, enough to pierce to the soul anyone with a soul to be pierced ? ... he still looms over the world, his message still clear, his pity still infinite, his consolation still effective, his words still full of glory, wisdom and love.[39]

One of my favourite descriptions of the character of Jesus comes from the former Lord Chancellor, Lord

Hailsham. In his autobiographical *The Door Wherein I Went* he describes how the person of Jesus came alive to him when he was at university:

> The first thing we must learn about him is that we should have been absolutely entranced by his company. Jesus was irresistibly attractive as a man ... What they crucified was a young man, vital, full of life and the joy of it, the Lord of life itself, and even more the Lord of laughter, someone so utterly attractive that people followed him for the sheer fun of it ... the Twentieth Century needs to recapture the vision of this glorious and happy man whose mere presence filled his companions with delight. No pale Galilean he, but a veritable Pied Piper of Hamelin who would have the children laughing all round him and squealing with pleasure and joy as he picked them up.[40]

Here was someone who exemplified supreme unselfishness but never self pity; humility but not weakness; joy but never at another's expense; kindness but not indulgence. He was a person in whom even his enemies could find no fault and where friends who knew him well said he was without sin. Surely no one could suggest that a man with a character like that was evil or unbalanced?

4.4 His fulfilment of Old Testament prophecy

Wilbur Smith, the American writer on theological topics, said:

> The ancient world had many different devices for determining the future, known as divination, but not in the entire gamut of Greek and Latin literature, even though they used the words prophet and prophecy, can we find any real specific prophecy of a great historic event to come in the distance future, nor any prophecy of a Saviour to arrive in the human race ... Mohammedanism cannot point to any prophecies of the coming of Mohammed uttered hundreds of years before his birth. Neither can the founders of any cult in this country rightly identify any ancient text specifically foretelling their appearance. [41]

Yet in the case of Jesus, he fulfilled over 300 prophecies (spoken by different voices over 500 years), including twenty-nine major prophecies fulfilled in a single day – the day he died. Although some of these prophecies may have found fulfilment at one level in the prophet's own day, they found their ultimate fulfilment in Jesus Christ.

I suppose it could be suggested that Jesus was a clever con man who deliberately set out to fulfil these prophecies in order to show that he was the Messiah foretold in the Old Testament.

The problem with that suggestion is, first, the sheer number of them would have made it extremely difficult. Secondly, humanly speaking he had no control over many of the events. For example, the exact manner of his death was foretold in the Old Testament (Isaiah 53), the place of his burial and even the place of his birth (Micah 5:2). Suppose Jesus had been a con man wanting to fulfil all these prophecies. It would have been a bit late by the time he discovered the place in which he was supposed to have been born!

4.5 His resurrection/conquest of death

The physical resurrection from the dead of Jesus Christ is the cornerstone of Christianity. But what is the evidence that it really happened? I want to summarise the evidence under four main headings.

i. His absence from the tomb

Many theories have been put forward to explain the fact that Jesus' body was absent from the tomb on the first Easter Day, but none of them is very convincing.

First, it has been suggested that Jesus did not die on the cross. There was once a headline in a major UK newspaper: 'Jesus did not die on the cross'. Dr Trevor Lloyd Davies claimed that Jesus was still alive when he was taken from the cross and that he later recovered.

Jesus had undergone a Roman flogging, under which many died. He had been nailed to a cross for six hours. Could a man in this condition push away a stone weighing probably a ton and a half? The soldiers were clearly convinced that he was dead or they would not have taken his body down. If they had allowed a prisoner to escape, they would have been liable to the death penalty.

Furthermore, when the soldiers discovered that Jesus was already dead, 'one of the soldiers pierced Jesus' side with a spear, bringing a sudden flow of blood and water' (John 19:34). This appears to be the separation of clot and serum which we know today is strong medical evidence that Jesus was indeed dead.

Secondly, it has been argued that the disciples stole the body. Some have suggested that the disciples stole the body and began a rumour that Jesus had risen from the dead. Leaving aside the fact that the tomb was guarded, this theory is psychologically improbable. The disciples were depressed and disillusioned at the time of Jesus' death. It would have taken something extraordinary to transform the apostle Peter into the man who preached at Pentecost when 3,000 people were converted.

In addition, when one considers how much they had to suffer for what they believed (floggings, torture, and for some even death), it seems inconceivable that they would be prepared to endure all that for something they knew to be untrue. I have a friend who was a scientist at Cambridge University who became a Christian because, as he examined the evidence, he was convinced that the disciples would not have been willing to die for what they knew to be a lie.

Thirdly, some have said that the authorities stole the body. This seems the least probable theory of all. If the authorities had stolen the body, why did they not produce it when they were trying to quash the rumour that Jesus had risen from the dead?

Perhaps the most fascinating piece of evidence relating to Jesus' absence from the tomb is John's description of the grave-clothes. In a way, the 'empty tomb' is a misnomer. When Peter and John went to the tomb they saw the grave-clothes which were, as the Christian apologist Josh McDowell put it in *The Resurrection Factor*, 'like the empty chrysalis of a caterpillar's cocoon' – when the butterfly has emerged.[42] It was as if Jesus had simply passed through the grave-clothes. Not surprisingly, John 'saw and believed' (John 20:8).

ii. His appearances to the disciples

Were these hallucinations? The Concise Oxford Dictionary describes a hallucination as an 'apparent perception of an external object not actually present'.

Hallucinations normally occur in highly strung, highly imaginative or very nervous people, or in people who are sick or on drugs. The disciples do not fit into any of these categories. Burly fishermen, tax collectors and sceptics like Thomas are unlikely to hallucinate. People who hallucinate would be unlikely suddenly to stop doing so. Jesus appeared to his disciples on eleven different occasions over a period of six weeks. The number of occasions and the sudden cessation make the hallucination theory highly improbable.

Furthermore, over 500 people saw the risen Jesus. It is possible for one person to hallucinate. Maybe it is possible for two or three people to share the same hallucination. But is it likely that 500 people would all share the same hallucination?

Finally, hallucinations are subjective. There is no objective reality – it is like seeing a ghost. Jesus could be touched, he ate a piece of broiled fish (Luke 24:42-43) and on one occasion he cooked breakfast for the disciples (John 21:1-14). Peter says, '[They] ate and drank with him after he rose from the dead' (Acts 10:41). He held long conversations with them, teaching them many things about the kingdom of God (Acts 1:3).

iii. The immediate effect

The fact of Jesus rising from the dead, as one would expect, had a dramatic impact on the world. The church was born and grew at a tremendous rate. As Michael Green, writer of many popular and scholarly works puts it:

> [The] church ... beginning from a handful of uneducated fishermen and tax gatherers, swept across the whole known world in the next three hundred years. It is a perfectly amazing story of peaceful revolution that has no parallel in the history of the world. It came about because Christians were able to say to inquirers: 'Jesus did not only die for you. He is alive! You can meet him and discover for yourself the reality we are talking about!' They did, and joined the church and the church, born from that Easter grave, spread everywhere. [43]

iv. Christian experience

Countless millions of people down the ages have experienced the risen Jesus Christ. They consist of people of every colour, race, tribe, continent and nationality. They come from different economic, social and intellectual backgrounds. Yet they all unite in a common experience of the risen Jesus Christ. Wilson Carlile, who was head of the Church Army in this country, was preaching at Hyde Park Corner. He was saying, 'Jesus Christ is alive today.' One of the hecklers shouted out to him, 'How do you know?' Wilson Carlile replied, 'Because I was speaking to him for half an hour this morning!' Millions of Christians could say the same today.

CONCLUSION

Jesus says in John 14:6, 'I am the Way, the Truth and the Life.' It is for each of us to decide if we believe him. The Gospels, the book of Acts and the Epistles make it clear that the earliest Christians believed Jesus to be both God and fully human. The task of the early church was to work out and express in precise terms the theological truth implied by these facts.

The apostle Paul and the earliest Christian writers were more concerned to insist on the reality of both the godhood and the manhood of Christ than to attempt to interrelate them. It was only when one-sided distortions of the truth came into being, such as the Gnostic view that there was no real assumption of humanity, that the apologists of the second century began elaborating on the implications of the Incarnation.

The early controversies were finally settled at the Council of Chalcedon in 451AD with the formulae: 'one and the same Son...the same perfect in godhead and the same perfect in manhood, truly God and truly man...like us in all things except sin.' [44] This has been accepted as the classical definition of orthodox Christian belief. The truth is that Jesus did die for our sins and that forgiveness is possible. He rose again from the dead and death is defeated. These facts transformed the lives of the early Christians. It is a message for which many of the apostles and thousands of others were willing, and are still willing, to suffer, be tortured and die. It is a message which transformed the ancient world, transforms our world today, and indeed transformed my own life. Over the last 30 years I have experienced God's love, his power and the reality of a relationship with him. I for one am convinced that Jesus rose from the dead and is alive today.

The evidence that Jesus rose from the dead is very extensive. A former Chief Justice of England, Lord Darling, said, 'In its favour as living truth there exists such overwhelming evidence, positive and negative, factual and circumstantial, that no intelligent jury in the world could fail to bring in a verdict that the resurrection story is true.' [45]

We saw when we looked earlier in the booklet at what Jesus said about himself that there were only three realistic possibilities – either he was and is the Son of God, or else deluded or something more sinister. When one looks at the evidence it does not make sense to say that he was insane or evil. The whole weight of his teaching, his works, his character, his fulfilment of Old Testament prophecy and his conquest of death make those suggestions absurd, illogical and unbelievable. On the other hand, they lend the strongest possible support to Jesus' own consciousness of being a man whose identity was God.

In conclusion, as C.S. Lewis pointed out: 'We are faced then with a frightening alternative.' Either Jesus was (and is) exactly what he said, or else he was insane or something worse. To C.S. Lewis it seemed clear that he could have been neither insane nor evil and thus he concludes, 'However strange or terrifying or unlikely it may seem, I have to accept the view that he was and is God.' [46]

The truth about Jesus is so much more wonderful and exciting than the myths. *The Da Vinci Code* says that the church has been hiding the real truth about Jesus and that this is the greatest conspiracy of the last 2,000 years. However, I want to ask whether it is *The Da Vinci Code* which is hiding the real truth about Jesus, the truth that has the power to change lives. The myths do not have this power. The message of orthodox Christianity has the power to set people free from compulsions and addictions, to reunite husbands and wives, parents and children and to change communities. The myths are so deadly dull in comparison with orthodox Christianity. As G.K. Chesterton put it:

> People have fallen into a foolish habit of speaking of Orthodoxy as something heavy, humdrum, and safe. There never was anything so perilous or so exciting as Orthodoxy. It was sanity: and to be sane is more dramatic than to be mad... To have fallen into any of those open

traps of error and exaggeration which fashion after fashion and sect after sect set along the historic path of Christendom – that would indeed have been simple. It is always simple to fall; there are an infinity of angles at which one falls, only one at which one stands. To have fallen into any one of the fads from Gnosticism to Christian Science would indeed have been obvious and tame. But to have avoided them all has been one whirling adventure.[47]

NOTES:

1. *The Daily Telegraph*, 3 October 2004.

2. *The New York Times*, 17 March 2003.

3. Mark Greene, 'Cracking the Code', London Institute for Contemporary Christianity available at http://www.licc.org.uk /articles/article.php/id/130

4. Carl Olson and Sandra Meisel, *The Da Vinci Hoax – Exposing the Errors in The Da Vinci Code* (Ignatius Press, 2004), p.296.

5. Cardinal George, Foreword to *The Da Vinci Hoax – Exposing the Errors in The Da Vinci Code* (Ignatius Press, 2004), p.11.

6. Dan Brown, *The Da Vinci Code* (Corgi, 2003), p.318.

7. *The Da Vinci Code*, p.342.

8. *The Da Vinci Code*, p.15.

9. From the Official Website of Dan Brown: www.danbrown.com/novels/davinci_code/faqs.html

10. Dan Brown, *The Da Vinci Code* (Corgi, 2003), p.331.

11. *The Da Vinci Code*, p.317.

12. *The Da Vinci Code*, p.343.

13. James M. Robinson (ed.) *The Nag Hammadi Library* (Harper San Francisco, 1977, 1990), p.138.

14. *The Da Vinci Code*, p.148.

15. Dan Brown, *The Da Vinci Code* (Corgi, 2003), p.333.

16. *The Da Vinci Code*, p.334.

17. *The Da Vinci Code*, p.317.

18. Pliny, *Letters*, Book X, 96 c.112

19. Ignatius of Antioch, *Letter to the Ephesians*, chapter 15.

20. Justin Martyr, *Dialogue with Trypho*, chapter 126.

21. Melito of Sardis, fragment in Anastasius of Sinai's *The Guide*, p.13.

22. Irenaeus, *Against Heresies*, Book 3, chapter 29:1, 2.

23. Clement of Alexandria, *Exhortation to the Greeks* 1:7:1.

24. Tertullian, *The Soul*, 41:3.

25. J.N.D. Kelly, *Early Christian Doctrines* (Adam and Charles Black, 1980), p.138.

26. Dan Brown, *The Da Vinci Code* (Corgi, 2003), p.315.

27. *The Da Vinci Code*, p.316.

28. *The Da Vinci Code*, p.313.

29. Nicene Creed.

30. Dan Brown, *The Da Vinci Code* (Corgi, 2003), p.315.

31. *The Da Vinci Code*, p.313.

32. F.F. Bruce, *The New Testament Documents – Are They Reliable?* (InterVarsityPress 1981), p.22.

33. F.J.A. Hort, The New Testament in the Original Greek, Vol.1, page 561 (New York: Macmillan Co).

34. Sir Frederic Kenyon, *The Bible and Archaeology* (Harper and Row, 1940).

35. Josephus, Antiquities, XVIII 63f. Even if, as some suggest, the text has been corrupted, none the less the evidence of Josephus confirms the historical existence of Jesus.

36. CS Lewis, *Mere Christianity* (Fount, 1952).

37. *Ibid*

38. Bernard Ramm, *Protestant Christian Evidence* (Moody Press).

39. By kind permission of Bernard Levin

40. Lord Hailsham, *The Door Wherein I Went* (Fount/Collins, 1975).

41. Wilbur Smith, *The Incomparable Book* (Beacon Publications, 1961).

42. Josh McDowell, *The Resurrection Factor* (Here's Life Publishers).

43. Michael Green, *Evangelism through the Local Church* (Hodder & Stoughton, 1990).

44. Council of Chalcedon

45. Michael Green, *Man Alive* (InterVarsity Press, 1968).

46. C.S Lewis, *Surprised by Joy* (Fontana, 1955).

47. G.K Chesterton, 'Orthodoxy', in *The Collected Works of G.K.Chesterton*, vol I (San Francisco: Ignatius Press, 1986), p.305-306.

If you would like to find
out about an Alpha course
near you, see the website
alpha.org

Alpha